Words From the Liberated and Content

poems by

Susan Stevens

Finishing Line Press
Georgetown, Kentucky

Words From the Liberated and Content

ACKNOWLEDGMENTS

My thanks to the editor of the online journal *Voices on the Wind*, in which
several of these poems, or versions thereof, appeared.

Cover art title is from an ancient rhyme often repeated by mariners:
"Red sky at night, sailors' delight.
Red sky at morning, sailors take warning."

Publisher: Leah Huete de Maines
Editor: Christen Kincaid
Cover Art: *Sailors' Delight* by Penny Duncklee (www.pennyduncklee.com)
Author Photo: Mario Acevedo
Cover Design: Elizabeth Maines McCleavy

Order online: www.finishinglinepress.com
also available on amazon.com

Author inquiries and mail orders:
Finishing Line Press
PO Box 1626
Georgetown, Kentucky 40324
USA

Contents

Alone I came into the world; alone I shall go from it....

Hermit Songs, texts written by 9th-13th century monks

*Aloneness has a beauty and grandeur.... One comes alone,
one goes alone....*

*If you silently sit with a tree...the tree is silent, you are silent...
and two silences cannot remain separate.... Whenever you feel
sad, sit by the side of a tree, by the side of the river, by the side
of a rock.... The more you relax, the more you will become
acquainted with the beauties of sadness.*

Osho, *Love, Freedom, Aloneness* (2001)

Nearly Everyone Looks Like You

That guy in the next car
has your beard
has your hairline—

And the fellow
with your face
who's wearing all black
at the next table
in the library
just has to be you.

If only he
would speak up
I'd know at once
if he was you.
But this group of his speaks
sotto voce as if
they mean to hide
a certain inflection...
their vocal timbre...
and vocabulary

I once saw someone
with your height and profile
in the health food store,
so ducked down
the next aisle
since the only place
I want to see you
is in my mind's eye

Paper Man

You are like the man I admire
in a novel but can't see,
albeit a man of many pictures
on flat paper (but a standout!)
and whom I know in books
and letters only. A man with whom
I've never uttered a coexistent word
but instead thrown myself at
with poem after poem.
The affection is deep
profound
indelible
pervading
penetrating
absorbing
electric
for my paper man

Roused at 1 AM

You called them *letters*,
I remembered, as I was falling asleep
then got up to write this poem.
How like you to use
the atypical term
for electronic intercourse
the finesse that woke me up
as is your wont
(you have done that a lot)

I find myself craving
a new book of yours...
It will both accentuate
and attenuate
our deep interval

Words from the Liberated and Content

Hearing from you
means the difference between
my wearing a general malaise
and falling asleep while smiling.

I am smiling now
because you are a silly
goose to call me *liberated*
with all its baggage and cliches—

But then again, I *am* liberated
to be able to love you
at constant distance
without making a show

of it. It was good of Donne
to say this to his bride:
For I would rather owner bee
    Of thee one houre, than all else ever.
Even Donne demanded
more than words: a presence.
But I hang on your words;
whatever can that mean?

Lining the wall beside my bed,
your pictures watch over like
sentinels or handsome chaperones,
I sometimes think, and sleep *content*.

**To one whose mystery is delicious
 and *sans peur et sans reproche***

Something I liked
about our words
was the way you kept me
off balance and
getting the hang
of language—no,
learning the hard way.

You, walking history-&-culture lesson—
keeping at a giant's stride beyond
so I could do some serious
cramming without cracking
a book. And never having
caught so much as a glimpse
of you. So much the better,
since as Charlie Chan tells us,
Distance no hindrance to fond thoughts.
There are times I won't share
the sound of ice loosening from its floe
or the rupture of a branch

Persona in Absentia

I have loved a man
never spoken to
except in writing.
Never touched, even
to shake his hand.
Or been in his presence, or
even within hundreds of miles.

Distance takes precedence
over repetition and tedium.
And vanity.

Neither timorous nor
unversed, I find the riot
of pictures on a wall
beside my bed
quite adequate,
thank you—and just
the ticket in times
of a viral pandemic
that insists
on the fatality
of getting close

Sleep Speech

When you wake up saying
"Mother," you wonder
whatever else you said
aloud in REM sleep—

Waking with a clean slate, brain's
toxic proteins cleared away
but, on the other hand,
emotional memory preserved
and language ability deepened,
—which doesn't explain the babbling
of a sleepwalker or sleeptalker.

At 19 on a train on the way
to Austin and my father's funeral
I did a somnambulist's walk
at night to the opposite end
of the car, saying, "Daddy,
Daddy—" and was walked back
to my seat by a Texan
with a Stetson who then
foully chose to press
his advantage
by trying to kiss me.

From then on I believed *menacing*
could be sensibly broken down
to its indubitable base word
expanding my language skills
enhanced by the power of REM

Breaking Through Ice

I know you wrote that poem but
it came from a different place.
Susan's writing self is more real
than the corporeal one

I feel it resonating now—
Once, I went into the writing
and haven't come out since

John Barth said:
The story of our life
is not our life; it is our story.

As Long As I Know You're There

We needn't meet over coffee
or in the library
at a poetry reading
the Iditarod
the Guggenheim
or Museum of Modern Art.
Because I see you in my head
and you are still writing
still orating

Your essence perpetuates
over the separation
that some would despise
but I favor
because it's more acute
brainy
affecting
as long as I know you're there
somewhere

Fable for T. M.
(near Thumb Butte in Prescott, 1985)

Sidestepping downed trees,
amassing boulders
in fantasy-fortress style,
I watch your stony face
and a form made erect
by the getting, and lean
by the wanting;
and I can view a mind
set by solitude
so that reaching
and withdrawal are equally easy;
and I can say the mystery
of walking these leaves
hazards the buzz
of your manufactured high

Paean

When I think that being alone
has always occupied a glorified place in my head,
then at 42 hearing your words: *I wish you'd ask me
to do more for you*, I see that acting singly
is no more noble than that interdependence
which we have. The exalted loner
can be much made over, even deified—
yet has but a handhold on the scale
we reach relying on one another.
Praise for solitary life is exaggerated.
How can I truly celebrate it in the midst
of your possessions? Your clothes surround me in riotous
multicolor, books flagged and waiting as you head to Sewanee;
the imprint of your touch on my arm remains.
Your absence gives pause to our readings—
suspended literary arch—confounding,
self-contradictory (you are all places),
conjuring up the way things are
on hikes on rides in groups alone at a gig on a job
with a book with a song/without it
in a clinch at rest ambling at a run in crisis in repose
looking at the outside the inside track of one another
seeing allowing the labor possible only
when engaged with someone else

Song at Dusk

Who says that trembling obtains
only in the confidant's presence?
I tremble at thoughts of you,
who are so far removed that
our not meeting is guaranteed.
It's good to know I can't
go white or dumb or ungrounded
in that dimension of what does
or doesn't come next

Where You and I Stand

The women who have been intimate
with you are enviable
but I don't envy them:
my preference is for words
(though I am on intimate terms
with my bassoon)

You are the man
I never want to put my hands on
the man in a passel of poems
I commune with, the man
whose letters comprise an unpublishable
piece of prose that is passionate enough,

the man in the doorway
with his hands on his hips
who says "Uh-huh"
to all that I've said

Retention

Good memories are lost jewels.
Valery

You are always here
with my canny skill for
instant replay
replay
replay

Your pictures are the cue
cards to bethink oneself
but I know you by heart

From Her Fortyish Daughter

1987

I, your nomadic daughter
who has been well-schooled by family
in wanderlust, find myself at that
crux where one more locale makes not
a whit of difference, only that you
have always been my point of reference.

Remembering the porch light that seemed
to have a short when the young men brought me home,
blinking don't-sit-out-there-come-in,
and your enlightened appraisal of all men,
I salute your equanimity, your handling
of all things domestic and artistic, your investing
of sensitivity in three ladies who
have always cried and laughed with ease.

This giving of yours has an opulence,
it holds a certain affirmation,
and my awe to see you persevere
cannot be gainsaid. We persist to wander,
and you continue to persist. Loving you
carries an elegance about it.

Dalliance

Why do I walk away if you play the libertine?
Because like Candide, I'd rather not judge—
(Since like Bartleby, *I would prefer not to*)
And it is the only venue in which I don't ask "why?"

Sagacity

Why castigate a man who walks among women
As if sampling at a county fair, or blame his dalliance—
Condemn him any more than those who tire
Of their life's work or what they wear?
If you must sometime be a judge,
A sense of equity trumps the letter of the law.

It Never Obliges

You are the man I admire
at long distance because
that distance maintains
the admiration; because
it gives me more time
than your presence would
to think about you.
Why is thinking more pleasing?
Because it avoids repetition
of behavior, talk,
and expectation. I think
when I read your poems.
I think when I read your mail
(and the reply), and I think
of how animating your pictures are,
rightly on the wall, inanimate
and the incredulity of that man
in those pictures writing those words

Stopping Time

*The camera is an excuse to be someplace you otherwise
don't belong.*
Susan Meiselas

Looking at photos of people
I'm the one who's always dying
to know who took the picture,
seeing as how expressions range
from seductive to indifferent
to caught-off-guard to modest
to fatuous to vain

Look at that man smiling
in his doorway
he looks delicious
making me wish I'd been
behind the camera.
And the photographer
included a fantastic black
knocker on the door.

We wonder what
she just said
to evoke the man's
aspect. And what unutterable
thing is it one wants
from a static image?

Rear Window

This U-shaped, multistory building
reminds me of the movie
and the main character's room
where I expect to look out
and across the grassy strip to see
(with some difficulty, sans James Stewart's
binoculars) Raymond Burr in one window
arguing with his filmic wife
and a woman letting her dog down
in a basket to the ground.

But now, there's a red light in one window,
a cat in another, and (much obliged!)
no fighting couples shouting profanities
in this over-55 community, and
no giggling, screaming children.

Try as I might to imagine
the comparison complete,
this place I live isn't ominous,
there is no seamy underside
(everything out in the open,
including propriety and aging)—
instead I feel safe, barring
a freakish southwest tornado or earthquake.

To think that a film could captivate
so enduringly, the Hitchcock effect
etched in one's sensibility
and revived in the innocuous
view that has now metamorphosed
doggedly in its horrific
climb to my third-floor window.

Susan **Stevens** has taught composition, literature, and creative writing on the Navajo reservation at Many Farms and at campuses in Tennessee, Georgia, and Arizona, including Yavapai College and Eastern Arizona College, where she partnered with the Arizona Commission on the Arts to direct the Visiting Writing Series. She received a bachelor's in comparative literature from the University of Redlands and a master's in creative writing under the tutelage of iconoclastic poet Jim Simmerman, late Regents' Professor at Northern Arizona University. Finishing Line Press published her poetry collection *Things We Might Miss* (2017) and chapbooks *With Ridiculous Caution* (2013) and *O, But in the Library* (2017). A retired educator and federal employee, she is presently a freelance writer-editor in New Mexico.

www.ingramcontent.com/pod-product-compliance
Lightning Source LLC
LaVergne TN
LVHW041330080426
835513LV00008B/663